ACTION PLAN FOR RELEASE

Nicolasa A. Gonzalez

authorHOUSE®

AuthorHouse™
1663 Liberty Drive
Bloomington, IN 47403
www.authorhouse.com
Phone: 833-262-8899

Published by AuthorHouse 08/29/2022

ISBN: 978-1-5246-9374-9 (sc)
ISBN: 978-1-5246-9373-2 (e)

Library of Congress Control Number: 2017908245

Print information available on the last page.

Any people depicted in stock imagery provided by Thinkstock are models,
and such images are being used for illustrative purposes only.
Certain stock imagery © Thinkstock.

This book is printed on acid-free paper.

CONTENTS

PURPOSE

The purpose of this workbook is to:

- Present a simple time-management tool to help you achieve your day-to-day goals. The time-management tools are arranged in a 30-day calendar with goals broken out by category.

- Help you—as someone recently incarcerated in county jail or prison—to develop and follow a plan of action that you have created for yourself.

- Provide a format to follow either starting 30 days prior to release from county jail or prison or starting with the release.

- Ensure that you have a workable plan of action at the time of your release back into the community.

- Inform you of places where you need to go and people you need to contact to assist you in achieving what you need to accomplish to return to being a healthy and productive member of society.

- Enable you to help yourself with first steps in an action plan upon being released from incarceration.

HOW TO USE THIS WORKBOOK

Action Plan for Release is a self-help book in a workbook format to guide you through the challenges that you face upon being released from incarceration. This workbook shows you how to use time-management tools and a monthly calendar to help you plan and prepare for the things that you need to accomplish to make your transition back into society successful, including tips for your daily routine. Many mandatory requirements for recently incarcerated individuals may seem overwhelming. They may seem like too much to do, especially right after having been locked up! You may have to go to meetings, receive counseling services, get your urine tested (through a urinanalysis or UA), look for a job, sign up for job training, or take steps to get your general equivalency diploma (GED) or to enroll in college courses. And these are just some examples of what you may be required to do.

The best way to succeed in this transition is to wrap your mind around the tasks that you need to accomplish before you set out to do them. If you are prepared in your mind for what is expected of you, it will be easier for you to stay on track. Here is an example:

> Your friend Mary is throwing a party in a few days—on Friday night. She wants you to help her plan it, so you talk with her about the decorations, as well as the food and beverages that you will be serving. You make a grocery list of what you will need to buy at the store. You can visualize how the party will look, how the food will taste, and the guests you would like to invite. You think about getting a new outfit for the event, even the shoes you would like to wear. The main thing is that you can see yourself going through all the steps that you would need to carry out to make the event happen the way you would like it to go.

Preparing for this party with your friend is similar to what this workbook covers: getting you to think ahead of time of all the things that you would need to do for things to go smoothly and according to the outcome that you desire. This workbook will explain how you can make a calendar and break goals down into the specific steps you would need to take on any given day. There will be a page with an example to explore this idea further. Managing your time effectively is a crucial part of making your transition successfully. After what you've been through already, it may at first be hard for you to imagine following a routine and a basic schedule. You can do it!

Keep in mind that the most important aspect of changing your life for the better lies in changing the way you think. You may need to do some things that feel hard to do, including distancing yourself from the friends of yours who continue to drink and to use drugs. If you keep hanging out with them, this is almost certainly going to lead to your downfall, so you need to face certain risks and make the tough choices that will serve you best in the long run. You will probably need to change many things about your surroundings: where you go, people you spend time with, and activities that were a part of your life in the past. Choose wisely the organizations and groups that you join. Choose ones that will encourage you to make good choices and to stay on track, whether these are religious institutions, community organizations, self-help groups, or 12-Step programs. Your goal should be to interact with people who faced the same problems and situations that you have encountered who will support you in learning new ways of thinking about what you have been through so that you can develop the skills and new habits that will serve you best from now on. You will need to find people with whom you can speak frankly about what you've been through and issues that you are facing now. You want to maximize your chances of success, and you don't have to do every single thing on your own. It's OK to share with others who can share their own experience, strength, and hope in ways that will help you.

If you are sick and tired of feeling hopeless and feel that your life is going nowhere, this workbook is here to help you take some first steps in turning your life around. To turn your life around, you will need to be the one to take charge of your own life. You will need to work hard at this. You will need determination and focus. You will need to work as hard at turning your life in a positive direction as you used to work at obtaining alcohol or drugs. The good news is that if you really want to get your life back, you can.

QUESTIONS TO ASK YOURSELF

You may feel overwhelmed, but you do not have to do everything all at once. You may ask yourself these questions to help figure out what you need to do right away:

1. Do I need to report to Probation & Parole? Drug Court? Pre-Trial Services? The Community Custody Program (CCP)? Or any other program?
2. Do I need to contact the New Mexico Children, Youth & Families Department (CYFD)?
3. Have I applied for assistance, including food stamps. Temporary Aid to Needy Families (TANF), and subsidized housing?
4. Do I need to sign up for counseling services?
5. Do I need a list of groups and meetings (including locations, days of the week, and times) for Alcoholics Anonymous (AA) or Narcotics Anonymous (NA)?
6. Where can I get a bus pass?
7. Do I need to enroll to get my general equivalency diploma (GED) or to enroll to attend college courses?
8. Do I need job training?
9. Do I need to obtain my birth certificate, my Social Security card, or my driver's license?
10. Do I have a place to go that provides me with a safe environment?
11. What is the most important thing that I have to take care of right now?

Now make your own list of things that you need to take care of. Begin with the most important ones. Keep this list so that you can refer to it later. When you accomplish a goal, you may put a line through it, which will help you track your achievements.

1. _____

2. _____

3. _____

4. _____

5. _____

6. _____

7. _____

8. _____

9. _____

10. _____

11. _____

12. _____

13. _____

14. _____

15. _____

16. _____

17. _____

18. _____

19. _____

20. _____

CREATING A PLAN OF ACTION

Agencies exist that can help you to obtain child support, enroll in general equivalency diploma (GED) courses, get a birth certificate or an identification card, or receive counseling or legal assistance. If you are a member of a Native tribe, services are available to you, and you could benefit from gaining access to them. If you are not sure what is available for you, ask. Keep asking until you find out whether you can get the help that you seek.

If you wish to attend meetings of Alcoholics Anonymous (AA) or Narcotics Anonymous (NA), the names of groups and the days, times, and locations are available online. Find a meeting that is suitable for you. If one particular meeting does not seem right for you, try another one. Find meetings on days, at times, and at locations that would work for you. Those public listings may or may not include the name and contact information (phone or email address) of someone you could contact with any questions. Once you know which meeting(s) you wish to attend, be sure to put the days and times on your calendar. This becomes part of your personal Action Plan for Release. Keeping track of meetings and appointments on your calendar (with relevant contact information in case you need to reschedule or cancel an appointment) will help you keep track of the commitments that you need to honor each day and each week. You may keep your calendar, list of meetings, and sign-in sheets in a three-ring binder to help you stay organized and keep on top of the documents that you will need.

In case your probation officer (or anyone else in authority) asks you to provide proof that you have been carrying out the tasks in your action plan, the three-ring binder's contents should help you to provide that proof. This workbook contains sheets for you and your sponsor to fill out and sign to provide proof that you're meeting with your sponsor. The binder lets you take out sheets when you need to show them to others and then store them safely again for future reference.

If you get discouraged about being able to do all the tasks required of you, I am here to tell you, "Yes, you can complete those tasks!" A lot depends on how you choose to think about and look at your own situation. Remind yourself of your desire to change your life when you feel overwhelmed or discouraged. Remember that there is always one way or another to find the answers that you need and to figure out how to get in touch with the people, organizations, and resources that you will need. Many resources are available on the Internet (for example, through searching on Google) or in phone directories (in print or online). Once you complete two weeks of the steps in your action plan, you may find it easier to get over the feeling that you're not getting anywhere. Every day, you can renew your faith in yourself and your Higher Power. This workbook is intended to be a tool to keep you on track, to keep things simple, and to help you stay organized.

The frustrations you experience with people, places, and things may tempt you to slip back into your old ways. You need to stay as strong and as level-headed as you can, but even if you are not perfect at this, you can still succeed! Your patience will be tested, including your patience with yourself. As long as you keep at it, one step at a time, one day at a time, you can succeed. You do not have to keep your feelings bottled up. If you know where to look, you can find others who will want you to succeed and who will be willing to listen to you when you need to blow off steam. You may find support with a counselor, a friend, a member of a religious group, or a support group for people in your situation. Recovery depends to a great extent on finding others who have been in the same situation (or a similar one) who have stayed on track and gotten through the process too. If you are tempted to go back to the old ways, it is better to share this temptation with others than to act on it. Others can show you that it is possible to stay clean and sober.

Now that you have made a list of the most important things that you need to take care of in your life, right now, at this moment, you can apply these things to a day-to-day calendar, starting with your date of release back into what some people refer to as "the real world."

EXAMPLE:

MONDAY

7:00 a.m.: Report to Pretrial Services
333 Lomas Blvd., NW, #120
Albuquerque, NM

7:00 p.m.–8:00 p.m.: Go to a meeting
of Narcotics Anonymous (NA)
St. Bernadette Church
on Indian School Road between Morris
and Juan Tabo
Albuquerque, NM

TUESDAY

7:30 a.m.: Get enrolled at Gordon
Bernell, 401 Roma, NW, 3rd floor
Albuquerque, NM

Contact counseling services for substance
abuse and relapse prevention.

6:30 p.m.: Sagebrush Living Free
6440 Coors Blvd, NW
Albuquerque, NM
(505) 922-9200
"Back on Track" Support Group

Action Plan For Release

conet w/plan 2/13

Sunday	Monday	Tuesday	Wednesday	Thursday	Friday	Saturday
	11 School 7:30 A.m - 3:00 p.m.	**12** School 7:30 A.m - 3:00 pm	**13** 9:00 A.m Court w/Judge Brown. Release Dad picks up. Report to Pre-trial	**14** Wake up 7:00 Am 8:00 Am Register my car. 10:00 Am Go to Brookeline Re-enroll. 11:00 AM Job search 1-2:00 Report to Pretrial, 7pm-NA	Go look at apts. Contact CYFD Report to pre-trial 1-2pm Job search 7pm NA meeting.	Search for apts Search for Job
Go to church Suboxone NA Meeting	Medical new treatment Pretrial Report 1-2pm 7pm NA meeting	Job search Until I find a Job. Report to pre-trial 1-2p.m 7pm NA meeting	Go to UNM care for suboxone & medical financial help. Job Search Report to pre-trial 1-2pm NA meeting 7pm	Job Search Report to Pre-trial 1-2pm NA meeting at 7pm	Job Search Report to Pre-trial 1-2pm NA meeting 7pm	Goal: Every weekend doing fun activity such as shopping, swimming etc... NA meeting
Church at Suboxone 7pm NA meeting	Start School at Brookeline 4 weeks til Graduation Report to pre-trial 1-2 p.m 7pm NA meeting	School at Brookeline 8-12 Report to pre-trial 4pm NA meeting Work	School 8-12p.m Report to Pre-trial 1-2pm 7pm NA meet. Work	School 8-12p.m Report to Pre-trial 1-2pm 7pm NA meet. Work	School 8-12pm Report to Pre-trial 1-2pm 7pm NA meet Work	Fun Pictures Work NA meeting 7pm
Church at Suboxone 7pm NA	School 8Am - 12p.m Report to Pre-trial 1-2pm	School 8Am-12p.m Report to Pre-trial 1-2p.m Work	School 8A.m - 12p.m Report to Pre-trial 1-2pm Work	School 8Am - 12pm Report to Pre-trial 1-2p.m Work	School 8-12pm Report to Pre-trial 1-2pm 7pm N.A Work	Fun Pictures Work NA meeting

To whom it may concern,

I was recently released from MDC 1-16-13, and since then I have been very successful in my recovery and I have a better outlook on my future. While I was incarcerated I attended the Action Plan for Release class which gave me resources for counseling and additional numbers which have helped me once I got out with my probation and myself. In addition, I was able to take my plan to my probation officer who was very happy to see I had a day by day plan she could visually see. I believe this program would be a great success for others. If there are any questions, feel free to call me at.

Action Plan For Release EXAMPle

Sunday	Monday	Tuesday	Wednesday	Thursday	Friday	Saturday
cember 16	Court date at 1:30	my mom will pick me up. If on Pre Trial or CCP will Report	Contact my counselor Leslie Wilson. Contact place of employment or Job apps	Contact La Entrada (SOS) 243-1556 For Substance abuse relapse Prevention	Put Job apps.	
	Go to school					Go to church
23	24 Contact Gordon Bernal to continue my education. Put Job apps	25 Report to CCP or Pre Trial	26 Go to counseling w/Leslie	27 Go to LA Entrada For meeting	28 Put Job apps. →	29
		Go to school	Go to school	Go to school		Go to church
30	31	January 1 Report to CCP or Pre Trial	2 Go to Counseling w/Leslie	3 LA Entrada meeting	4	5
		(Put Job applications) ← (Winter Break For School)		→		Go to Church
6 2 Entrada 09 Gold	7	8 (Put Job Applications) ←	9	10	11 →	12

To whom it may concern:

    While I was incarsarated I attended the Action Plan For Release Class, this class was very helpful for me, to Keep me focused upon Release, it helped me to make a plan for positive things that I would need to take care of in my daily life besides making a plan for the tasks that I would need to complete, it also had great resources; as far as Counseling angencies, food banks, shelter, and numbers that are neccessary to whelp you. This class can benifit inmates who need structure and can whelp them get on the right track and help them realize that their are many resources that many people do not know about and I believe this class can help them to succeed

       Thank You

Action Plan For Release EXAMPLE

Sunday	Monday	Tuesday	Wednesday	Thursday	Friday	Saturday
December 16	Court date at 2:30 ... Go to School [17]	My mom will pick me up. If on Pre Trial or CCP will Report [18]	Contact my counselor Leslie Hibari. Contact place of employment or Tribzaps [19]	Contact La Entrada (505) 243-1556 For Substance abuse relapse Prevention [20]	Put Job apps. [21]	[22] Go to church
[23]	Contact Gordon Bernel to continue my education. Put Job Apps [24]	Report to CCP or Pre Trial [25]	Go to Counseling w/ Leslie [26]	Go to La Entrada For meeting [27]	Put Job apps. [28]	[29]
[30]	[31] Go to School	January 1 Report to CCP or Pre Trial. Go to School	Go to Counseling w/ Leslie [2] Go to School	La Entrada meeting (3) Go to School	[4]	[5] Go to church
	(Put Job applications) (Winter Break For School)					Go to church
Entrada og Gold [6]	[7]	8	[9]	[10]	[11]	[12]
	(Put Job Applications)					

To whom it may concern:

   While I was incarserated I attended the Action Plan For Release class, this class was very helpful for me, to keep me focused upon release, it helped me to make a plan for positive things that I would need to take care of in my daily life besides making a plan for the tasks that I would need to complete, it also had great resources; as far as counseling angencies, food banks, shelter, and numbers that are necessary to help you. This class can benifit inmates who need structure and can help them get on the right track and help them realize that their are many resources that many people do not know about and I believe this class can help them to succeed.

                Thank You

SITUATIONS, ISSUES, OR CONCERNS FOR WHICH YOU COULD USE HELP

Situations will arise that will require your attention. You may need to get advice about how to handle a certain situation. You may list these situations—situations that make you feel frustrated or concerned—on this page so that you can ask for help.

1. _____

2. _____

3. _____

4. _____

5. _____

6. _____

7. _____

8. _____

9. _____

10. _____

11. _____

12. _____

13. _____

14. _____

15. _____

16. _____

17. _____

18. _____

19. _____

20. _____

21. _____

22. _____

23. _____

24. _____

25. _____

26. _____

27. _____

28. _____

29. _____

30. _____

31. _____

32. _____

33. _____

34. _____

35. _____

36. _____

37. _____

38. _____

39. _____

40. _____

ACTION PLAN FOR RELEASE

"We cannot become what we want by remaining what we are." —Max De Pree

1. Write down phone numbers, addresses, and times.
2. Make a list of the names of people you need to speak with directly.
3. Color code your calendar with highlighter pens of different colors. (For example, highlight all NA meetings in pink.)
4. Write down at least one goal to accomplish each day. When you have completed that goal, check it off or draw a line through it.
5. Be sure to write on your calendar all important appointments and deadlines.
6. You may make your calendar as colorful as you would like.
7. Be sure to write down the names of contact persons and/or agencies, phone numbers, and addresses, in addition to dates and times of appointments.

Action Plan for Release

We cannot become what we want by remaining what we are......Max De Pree

```
                    P X J E T N V Q R C
                  M J Z S I U X R W A R Z O N E J
                M O U F I Z J Z E U X E M A C C U P W E
              O N M G W A K C E H C E O H R D P R L O E V
            J L S P J B L A C K J M J S O S A G V R E G N N Y S
          B L T S T T R A N S I E N T R G A N G S H O D B H I V Z
        W Y E U B O D D R G H E T T O B I R D S S J B B N H L F S I
        H N R I V Y R Y E J M F I M Y A E G N A R O A U R A E O B N R Y
        C G T K O I G F         Z Q T O K U H D         D P T F F U O K
        S K G E E B Z Q H       N F C E D C F D         J G G I F R G C P
        N P T V B L J J B V      M O J R T T M B         S I E O O O V I Z R
        J R Z J I A X R B Q      D V I E E O L D         U B I V C N O S A F
        H P I T A B N I Z H C    M A R T W F D U         I N F I R M A R Y S E
        Z O S J B Q U F L V A    J T Y S A O I G         V W R C S C Z C C G K
        D W O V I S I T O R S    S S N C L R D L         A X A W O N V E Y P G
      P T V N R X S H M A U F    Q M B J A L E R         Y P T U M W O F G I S J
      Y E A R Y O A C B L Z A V K U U R G O I V L K R A V B S B V R I O E B U Z Q U A
      F X E O H A C D S Y Y F H H W F D F U P Z B L R A Y I M J T T V J N A O R K R C
      K G M L L D R K Y P M W H N K C O L B L L E C I S C A K H F N D F R G O Y R E K
      X T Z Z S G R W P F A M D B A G J V S Y L J O L D W N O X I T W D V X S E M W E
      P F E G E Y O U N G R R I T S E R R A E S U O H I A U I I G U A O L U S K C H T
      Q C D U O Z G O N W J Y O F E C O M M I S S A R Y S C Z A H V I S D T G E N B T
      P J M N G B R X Y K M M G L S X D S M I T C I V E L B L F T P E J T K O C E U Q
      L X W K N M   E G A T T T D E Q W R A B B I T E T A M L L E C K D   V C G F R B
      F Y E I A Y   L N C B A I E F U J X F U P A W G A N G S T E R S F   I J O X B F
        V C I V I     Y Q W M N D A F J O I N T B B W M C L U B F E D     O Z K L T
        C C A H P       N E A V K M J K I M D H Q V K M D E M R A F       L R O U L
      Y X O V M C                                                     D A R O W V
        G E I I A                                                     O L T Z L Q
        R V S P V G                                                   O U C I N A G
        I A R S C G                                                   M B O P O S I
        E A D X S E E                                                 T Q U N Y N B D
        A I X T A D H F S A R E H J H S W J Z D I W O H C X R S T X H J
        J Z E B L M P E M O U G K J F N H F Q C E V A W T A E H C U
        N D J V G F W O A Y J P K N I L C N P T A T T O O S T A
        D I I M N T I D K F S T O R E K E I S T E R Y P I B
        Q J C H A F D Z O X H Z C R I M I N I A L W N U
        N P C M O E J T L O Q B U S T O U T U S
        J S G G A Z F O S F C V L D C A
        I K V W S H W S P V
```

WORD LIST:

ARREST	DIME	JCAT	PRISON
BAIL	DRUNK TANK	JOINT	PROBATION
BLACK	FARM	JUDGE	RABBIT
BUG	FIGHT	JUMPSUIT	RAT
BUNKS	FREE	KEISTER	ROAD DOG
BUST OUT	GANGS	KOOL AID	ROCK
CADILLAC	GANGSTERS	LIFER	SNITCH
CELL BLOCK	GAS	LOCKDOWN	STORE
CELL MATE	GHETTO BIRD	MOLLY	STRETCH
CHOW	GLASS	MONSTER	TATTOOS
CLINK	GUARD	NORMAICY	TRANSIENT
CLUB FED	HEAT WAVE	OFFENDER	VICTIMS
COMMISSARY	HOE CHECK	OG	VIOLATION
CONFINE	HOUSE ARREST	ORANGE	VISITORS
COURT	INCARERATION	PAROLE	WARZONE
COURTHOUSE	INFIRMARY	PEELS	YARD
COWBOY	JACKET	PIMP	
CRIMINIAL	JAILBIRD	PO	

YOU CAN DO THIS!

You have completed the toughest part: thinking about the steps that you need to take first and making an action plan. Now it's time for you to get to work! Your action plan should give you at least one task to accomplish each and every day. This will help you to move towards your goals and stay productive. Remember: easy does it! Your life probably did not get into a big mess in a single day, and it probably won't get all better in a single day either. The problem of alcohol or drug abuse probably grew worse for you over a long period of time. The point is that somehow, you got off track and got off the path of being sober. Your life took a turn for the worse. This can happen so slowly and gradually that perhaps only when you look back can you see how over a period of years, you lost sight of your hopes and dreams. So don't be surprised or discouraged if it takes a while for you to get back on track through persistence and dedication.

You are bound to have days in which you don't feel as if you're making any progress. Focus on one task at a time, one day at a time, and remember that in doing that, you are taking charge of your life and making progress, even if it doesn't always feel that way. You are getting your life organized. You are reclaiming power over your life and its direction. Despite frustrations, remember to celebrate your accomplishments and successes. Pay attention to your thoughts. Remember: You don't have to believe every negative thought that pops into your head. Give yourself a pep talk and positive feedback for what you do manage to achieve to move toward your goals.

Explore new ideas, and surround yourself as much as you can with people who believe in you, care about you, and support your progress. Choose to be in the company of people who have overcome the problems that you have faced. They will help you believe that you can also overcome those problems. You can pick up new tips and develop new skills by hanging around these people and attending the support groups and recovery programs that that have helped them.

Remember to follow your plan each day, whether you feel like it or not on any given day. This is how people develop constructive habits. It may feel unfamiliar at first. You may feel discouraged at times. That is normal. You do not have to be perfect at this process for it to work for you in the long run. You do need to be honest with yourself and the people who are willing to help you. If you listen with an open mind to the people who are further ahead in their recovery than you are in yours, you are already ahead of the game. You may need to work on improving your self-discipline; you can do that if you are willing to do so. "Progress, not perfection." You can make progress. Anything is possible with willingness, determination, and persistence.

Good luck!

NA / AA MEETING VERIFICATION FORM

CLIENT NAME

Name	Location	Signature	Time	Date	Verified

NA / AA MEETING VERIFICATION FORM

CLIENT NAME

Name	Location	Signature	Time	Date	Verified

NA / AA MEETING VERIFICATION FORM

CLIENT NAME

Name	Location	Signature	Time	Date	Verified

SPONSOR MEETING VERIFICATION FORM

CLIENT NAME

Name	Location	Signature	Time	Date	Verified

SPONSOR MEETING VERIFICATION FORM

CLIENT NAME

Name	Location	Signature	Time	Date	Verified

SPONSOR MEETING VERIFICATION FORM

CLIENT NAME

Name	Location	Signature	Time	Date	Verified

Month-by-Month Calendar

Month				Year		
Sunday	Monday	Tuesday	Wednesday	Thursday	Friday	Saturday

Month-by-Month Calendar

_____ Month				_____ Year		
Sunday	Monday	Tuesday	Wednesday	Thursday	Friday	Saturday

Month-by-Month Calendar

	Month				Year	
Sunday	Monday	Tuesday	Wednesday	Thursday	Friday	Saturday

Month-by-Month Calendar

_____ Month				_____ Year		

Sunday	Monday	Tuesday	Wednesday	Thursday	Friday	Saturday

Month-by-Month Calendar

Month				Year		
Sunday	Monday	Tuesday	Wednesday	Thursday	Friday	Saturday

Month-by-Month Calendar

Month				Year		
Sunday	Monday	Tuesday	Wednesday	Thursday	Friday	Saturday

Month-by-Month Calendar

Month					Year	
Sunday	Monday	Tuesday	Wednesday	Thursday	Friday	Saturday

Month-by-Month Calendar

Month _____				**Year** _____		
Sunday	Monday	Tuesday	Wednesday	Thursday	Friday	Saturday

Month-by-Month Calendar

Month				**Year**		
Sunday	Monday	Tuesday	Wednesday	Thursday	Friday	Saturday

Month-by-Month Calendar

Month				Year		
Sunday	Monday	Tuesday	Wednesday	Thursday	Friday	Saturday

Month-by-Month Calendar

Month				**Year**		
Sunday	Monday	Tuesday	Wednesday	Thursday	Friday	Saturday

Month-by-Month Calendar

Month					Year	
Sunday	Monday	Tuesday	Wednesday	Thursday	Friday	Saturday

ABOUT THE AUTHOR

I am passionate about my own recovery and wish to help others, as others have helped me. At the age of 20 in 1996, I became addicted to crack, and I remained addicted for 15 years. I have learned in recovery to forgive myself for that chapter of my life and to be honest about it so that I can use my own experience to help others whose lives have taken a similar turn.

I grew up in an abusive home in the North Valley of Albuquerque, New Mexico. My mom had brought a man into our home who hurt me. I carried deep resentment about all of this and wanted nothing more than to escape the pain through alcohol and drugs. My use of alcohol and drugs came at a steep cost: I lost custody of my oldest daughter because I could not stop using. I was on the streets 24/7 looking for my next high, and it is hard even for me to believe the things that I was willing to do to get high. I regarded my addiction as my best friend. Several times, I almost killed myself.

I only sought help after the birth of my second child in 2004. I couldn't stand the pain that I was causing this child of mine. I feared that I would be unable to stop using crack and that I would lose my second child too. I realized that I would unless I stopped using alcohol and drugs completely. I put together a plan of action and followed it consistently and faithfully. I got counseling. I attended AA and NA meetings. I got active in Sagebrush Community Church. I bounced around between counseling, recovery programs, and jail for years. Getting clean and sober has been the biggest battle in my life, yet I have managed to get clean and sober and to stay clean and sober. I started doing little things one day at a time to get my life back on track. I was willing to do the things that I needed to do to stay sober, including gathering information and getting counseling. I went to support groups, including NA. I interacted with others in recovery from drug addiction. I could not have held onto being clean and sober for over 10 years now without the help that I received from others. The jail/prison ministries of Sagebrush Community Church have been particularly helpful for me.

If you have a sincere desire to get clean and sober, you can do it! What I've laid out in this workbook is a calendar plan of action like the one I used. It worked for me. It can work for you too. You can navigate Drug Court, the Community Custody Program (CCP), and Adult Probation. Help is available. It's up to you to take advantage of the programs and resources that can help you become and stay clean and sober. I hope that you are as willing as I have been to ask for help and to use what is out there that can help you.

Printed in the United States
by Baker & Taylor Publisher Services